God Is on
the Cross

DIETRICH BONHOEFFER

God Is on
the Cross

Reflections on Lent
and Easter

TRANSLATED BY O. C. DEAN JR.

COMPILED AND EDITED BY JANA RIESS

WESTMINSTER
JOHN KNOX PRESS
LOUISVILLE · KENTUCKY

Devotional text herein originally appeared in Dietrich Bonhoeffer's *I Want
to Live These Days with You: A Year of Daily Devotions* (Louisville, KY: Westminster
John Knox Press, 2007). Translated by O. C. Dean Jr. from the German *So will
ich diese Tag emit euch Leben* by Dietrich Bonhoeffer Jahreslesebuch published
in 2005 by Gütersloher Verlagshaus, Gütersloh, Germany.
Quotations as indicated are used by permission from Dietrich Bonhoeffer's *Meditations
on the Cross* (Louisville, KY: Westminster John Knox Press, 1998). Translated by
Douglas W. Stott from *Das Außerordentliche wird Ereignis: Kreuz und Auferstehung*,
published 1996 by Kaiser/ Gütersloher Verlagshaus, Gütersloh, Germany.

12 13 14 15 16 17 18 19 20 21 — 10 9 8 7 6 5 4 3 2 1

Book design by Drew Stevens
Cover design by Dilu Nicholas
Cover art: © Richard Lathulerie/istockphoto.com

Library of Congress Cataloging-in-Publication Data
Bonhoeffer, Dietrich, 1906–1945.
    [Selections. English. 2010]
    God is on the cross : reflections on Lent and Easter / by Dietrich Bonhoeffer ;
translated by O. C. Dean Jr. ; compiled and edited by Jana Riess.
        p. cm.
    Includes bibliographical references and index.
    ISBN 978-0-664-23849-0 (alk. paper)
    1. Lent — Meditations. 2. Easter — Meditations I. Riess, Jana. II. Title.
    BV85.B62513 2012
    242'.34 — dc23   2012011937

PRINTED IN THE UNITED STATES OF AMERICA

CONTENTS

TRANSLATOR'S PREFACE

Since Dietrich Bonhoeffer wrote before the days of inclusive gender, his works reflect a male-oriented world in which, for example, the German words for "human being" and "God" are masculine, and male gender was understood as common gender. In this respect, his language has, for the most part, been updated in accordance with the practices of the New Revised Standard Version of the Bible (NRSV); that is, most references to human beings have become gender-inclusive, whereas references to the Deity have remained masculine.

While scriptural quotations are mostly from the NRSV, it was necessary at times to substitute the King James Version (KJV), the Revised Standard Version (RSV), or a literal translation of Luther's German version, as quoted by Bonhoeffer, in order to allow the author to make his point. In a few other cases, the translation was adjusted to reflect the wording of the NRSV.

O. C. Dean Jr.

EDITOR'S PREFACE

This devotional brings together daily reflections from one of the twentieth century's most beloved theologians, Dietrich Bonhoeffer (1906–1945). These reflections have been chosen especially for Lent and Easter, a time when the liturgical calendar highlights several themes of Bonhoeffer's beliefs and teachings: that self-denial is a necessary aspect of a Christian life; that the cross is central to human understanding; and that, without the atonement, every one of us would stand forever in the role of Judas. Overall, the theme of suffering for Christ runs through Bonhoeffer's work as one of the "costs" of discipleship. "It is not the religious act that makes the Christian," he wrote, "but participation in the suffering of God in the life of the world."[1]

Although he came from a well-to-do family, by the time he wrote most of the content in this book, Bonhoeffer was well acquainted with suffering. Just two days after Adolf Hitler had seized control of Germany in early 1933, Bonhoeffer delivered a radio sermon in which he criticized the new regime and warned Germans that "the Führer concept" was dangerous and wrong. "Leaders of offices which set themselves up as gods mock God," his address concluded. But Germany never got to hear those final statements, because Bonhoeffer's microphone had been switched off mid-transmission.[2] This began a twelve-year struggle against Nazism in Germany, with Bonhoeffer running afoul of authorities and being arrested in 1943. Much of the content of this book was written during the two years he spent in prison.

For Bonhoeffer, waiting was a fact of life during the war: waiting to be released from prison; waiting to be able to spend more than an hour a month in the company of his young fiancée, Maria von Wedemeyer; waiting for the end of the war. In his absence, friends and former students were killed in battle and his parents' home was bombed; there was little he could do about any of this except pray and wield a powerful pen. Still he tried to live the words he wrote in this now-famous poem:

And if you hand us the heavy cup, the bitter one,
of sorrow, filled to the highest brim,
then we take it thankfully, without trembling,
from your good and loving hand.

For Bonhoeffer, the cup of sorrow may indeed have seemed heavy at times. When the Third Reich crumbled in April 1945, Hitler ordered the execution of some political prisoners who had conspired to overthrow him. Since papers had recently been discovered that confirmed Bonhoeffer's involvement in this anti-Nazi plot, the theologian was among those scheduled to be killed in one of Hitler's final executive decrees.[3] Bonhoeffer was hanged on April 8, 1945, just ten days before German forces began to surrender and less than three weeks before Hitler's own death by suicide. Bonhoeffer was thirty-nine years old. The camp doctor at Flossenbürg wrote this about the theologian's execution:

> On the morning of that day between five and six o'clock the prisoners . . . were taken from their cells and the verdicts of the court martial read out to them. Through the half-open door in one room of the huts I saw Pastor Bonhoeffer, before taking off his prison garb, kneeling on the floor praying fervently to his God. I was most deeply moved by the way this unusually lovable man prayed, so devout and so certain that God heard his prayer. At the place of execution, he again said a short prayer and then climbed the steps of the gallows, brave and composed. His death ensued after a few seconds. In the almost fifty years that I worked as a doctor, I have hardly ever seen a man die so entirely submissive to the will of God."[4]

Although Bonhoeffer's death (and the narrow timing of it) is tragic, we are fortunate that he was a prolific writer who left behind so many lectures, papers, letters, and diary entries from which we may piece together his theology.

HOW TO USE THIS BOOK

This book begins with Ash Wednesday and ends with Easter Sunday, encompassing the entire

Lenten season. Because the dates for Lent and Easter change each year, there are no calendar dates in this devotional, but you can easily find your place by knowing, for example, that it is the Saturday of the second week of Lent.

The weeks of Lent are arranged by theme — prayerful reflection, self-denial, temptation, suffering, and the cross — with a final series of devotions for Holy Week (Palm Sunday to Easter). Each day's devotion has a reflection from Dietrich Bonhoeffer, a Scripture to contemplate, and some bonus material. Although some of these additional short reflections come from other Christians throughout history, most of them are drawn from Bonhoeffer's own letters, sermons, and poetry, giving a glimpse of his attempt to live out a theology of Christian hope even when imprisoned and separated from family and beloved friends. It's important to remember how Bonhoeffer's beliefs were forged in the crucible of war and protest, and did not simply fall from the sky; it's equally important to recognize how intimately connected he was to those he loved.

PRAYERFUL REFLECTION

God Deceives No One

In the beginning, even before the start of his ministry, Jesus is tempted by the devil. The powers of evil, of falling away from God, approach him and try to bring him down at the very moment when he is assuming his role as Messiah (Luke 4:3–4). Luke reports that Jesus is famished, and then the devil confronts him: If you are the Son of God, tell this stone to become bread. If you have the power of God, then use it for yourself. Perform a miracle: turn the stone into bread, and you will be filled. Why, after all, do you have such power? If you are the Son of God, prove your power. . . . In this voice of apparent intercessory love, Jesus recognizes the voice of the devil. It was an outrageous suggestion, and he rejects the devil: "One does not live by bread alone, but by every word that comes from the mouth of God" (Matt. 4:4). Here that means basically: God deceives no one.

"And take up their cross." That cross is already there, ready, from the very beginning; we need only take it up. But to keep us from believing that we must simply choose any arbitrary cross, or simply pick out our suffering as we will, Jesus emphasizes that each of us has his or her *own* cross, ready, appointed, and appropriately measured by God.[1]

Dietrich Bonhoeffer, *The Cost of Discipleship*

Have mercy on me, O God,
    according to your steadfast love;
according to your abundant mercy
    blot out my transgressions.
Wash me thoroughly from my iniquity,
    and cleanse me from my sin.
For I know my transgressions,
    and my sin is ever before me.

Psalm 51:1–3

Prayer

The fact that we can pray is not something to be taken for granted. It is true that prayer is a natural need of the human heart, but that does not give us any right before God. . . . We pray to the God in whom we believe through Christ. Therefore our prayer can never be a conjuring up of God; we do not need to present ourselves before him. We can know that God knows what we need before we ask for it. That gives our prayer the greatest confidence and a happy certainty. It is neither the formula nor the number of words but faith that reaches God in his fatherly heart, which has long known us. The proper prayer is not a deed, not an exercise, not a pious attitude, but the petition of a child to the heart of the Father.

❖   ❖   ❖

We pray for the big things and forget to give thanks for the ordinary, small (and yet really not small) gifts.[2]

Dietrich Bonhoeffer, Life Together

❖ ❖ ❖

"And whenever you pray, do not be like the hypocrites; for they love to stand and pray in the synagogues and at the street corners, so that they may be seen by others. Truly I tell you, they have received their reward. But whenever you pray, go into your room and shut the door and pray to your Father who is in secret; and your Father who sees in secret will reward you."

Matthew 6:5–6

God Is Not a Matter of Mood

We say that religion is a matter of mood: we must wait until the mood strikes us. And then we often wait for years—perhaps until the end of our life—until we are once again in the mood to be religious. This idea is based on a great illusion. It is all well and good to let religion be a matter of mood but God is not a matter of mood. He is still present even when we are not in the mood to meet with him. . . . In religion, as in art and science, there are—in addition to times of great excitement—times of sober work and practice. Interaction with God must be practiced; otherwise we will not find the right tone, the right word, the right language, when he surprises us. We must learn God's language, laboriously learn it. And we must work at it, so that we will be able to talk with him.

❖ ❖ ❖

The morning prayer determines the day. Squandered time of which we are ashamed, temptations to which we succumb, weaknesses and lack of courage in work, disorganization and lack of discipline in our thoughts and in our conversation . . . all have their origin most often in the neglect of morning prayer. [3]

Dietrich Bonhoeffer, *Psalms*

❖　❖　❖

O LORD, in the morning you hear my voice;
    in the morning I plead my case to you, and watch.

Psalm 5:3

Meditation

In meditation it is not necessary for us to try to think and pray in words. Silent thinking and praying that comes from just listening can often be more beneficial. It is not necessary for us to find new ideas in meditation. Often that only distracts us and satisfies our vanity. It is quite enough for the word, as we read and understand it, to penetrate us and live within us. As the word of the shepherds moved Mary "in her heart" (Luke 2:51), as a person's word often stays in our minds, lives and works in us, occupies us, unsettles or delights us, without our being able to do anything about it, so in meditation God's word wants to enter us and remain with us. It wants to move us and work in us. . . . Above all, it is not necessary in meditation for us to have some kind of unexpected, extraordinary experiences. It can happen, but if it does not, that is not a sign that our meditation is futile. From time to time we will notice a great inner barrenness and indifference, a lack of interest and even incapability in meditation. We must not then get stuck in such experiences. Above all, we must not let them keep us—especially now—from holding to our meditation time with great patience and faithfulness.

❖   ❖   ❖

To be silent does not mean to be inactive; rather it means to breathe in the will of God, to listen attentively and be ready to obey.[4]

Dietrich Bonhoeffer, *Meditating on the Word*

❖   ❖   ❖

I will meditate on your precepts,
    and fix my eyes on your ways.
I will delight in your statutes;
    I will not forget your word.

Psalm 119:15–16

God Needs the Whole Heart

Those who have received God's word must begin to seek God. They can do no other. . . . We can seek God nowhere except in his word, but this word is alive and inexhaustible, for God himself lives in it. If God's word has found us, then we can say: "*With my whole heart* I seek you" (Ps. 119:10). For with half a heart we would seek an idol, but never God himself. God needs the whole heart. . . . But how easily we err when evil fogs our vision. We go astray and no longer know up from down or how to find our way back to the commandments of God. We must ask God daily to preserve us from the sin of straying, from unknowing sin (Num. 15:22–28), for if we ever stray unknowingly onto the path of evil, then we often quickly come to enjoy this path, and straying becomes evil intention. But those who seek God with their whole heart will not go astray.

My dearest Dietrich, every morning at six, when we both fold our hands in prayer, we know that we can have great faith, not only in each other but far, far above and beyond that. And then you can't be sad anymore either, can you? [5]

Maria von Wedemeyer to Dietrich Bonhoeffer
in Tegel prison, 24 May 1943

❖   ❖   ❖

With my whole heart I seek you;
    do not let me stray from your commandments.

Psalm 119:10

Hope Abides

A faith that does not hope is sick. It is like a hungry child who will not eat or a tired person who will not sleep. As certainly as people believe, so certainly do they hope. And it is no shame in hoping, in hoping boundlessly. Who would even want to talk of God and not hope? Who would want to talk of God without hoping one day to see him? . . . And why should we be ashamed of our hope? We will one day have to be ashamed, not of our hope, but of our miserable and anxious hopelessness that trusts nothing to God, that in false humility does not grasp where God's promises are given, that is resigned to this life and cannot look forward to God's eternal power and glory. The more people dare to hope, the greater they become with their hope: people grow with their hope—if it is hope only in God and his sole power. Hope abides.

The church is the place of unshakeable hope.[6]

Dietrich Bonhoeffer, "Confident Hope,"
sermon on 26 November 1933

❖ ❖ ❖

For surely I know the plans I have for you, says
the LORD, plans for your welfare and not for harm,
to give you a future with hope.

Jeremiah 29:11

God Can Wait

Human beings are the losers; God is the winner. God lets human beings start; he lets them make progress, have success, and seems himself to be totally passive. His countermoves seem rather insignificant, and we seldom notice them at all. So we march forward, proud and self-confident and certain of our success and ultimate victory. But God can wait; sometimes he waits year after year. . . . God waits in the hope that people will finally understand his moves and want to turn their life over to him. But once in every life—perhaps it will not be until the hour of death—God crosses our way, so that we can no longer take a step. We must stop and in fear and trembling recognize God's power and our own weakness and wretchedness. . . . Only in these great moments in our life do we understand the meaning of God's guidance in our life; only then do we understand God's patience and God's wrath. And only now do we recognize that these hours in which God crossed our way are the only hours of real importance in our life. They alone make our life worth living.

❖   ❖   ❖

Slowly it gets to be a waiting whose outward sense I cannot comprehend; the inward reason must be found daily. Both of us have lost infinitely much during the past months; time today is a costly commodity, for who knows how much more time is given to us.[7]

Dietrich Bonhoeffer to Maria von Wedemeyer,
20 September 1943

❖   ❖   ❖

So we do not lose heart. Even though our outer nature is wasting away, our inner nature is being renewed day by day. For this slight momentary affliction is preparing us for an eternal weight of glory beyond all measure, because we look not at what can be seen but at what cannot be seen; for what can be seen is temporary, but what cannot be seen is eternal.

2 Corinthians 4:16–18

SELF-DENIAL

Simple Obedience

When Jesus demanded voluntary poverty of the rich young man, the latter knew that there were only two choices: to obey or not to obey (Matt. 19:21). When Levi was called from his tax collecting and Peter from his nets, there was no doubt that Jesus was serious about his call. They were to leave everything and follow him (Mark 2:14; 1:16–17). When Peter is called onto the rolling sea, he has to get up and venture forth (Matt. 14:29). In all of this, only one thing was demanded: to rely on the word of Jesus Christ and accept his word as a more secure foundation than all the securities of the world. The powers that wanted to put themselves between the word of Jesus and obedience were just as great in those days as they are today. . . . The concrete call of Jesus and simple obedience have their irrevocable meaning. With it Jesus calls us in the concrete situation, in which he can be believed. He therefore calls concretely — and wants to be understood in just that way — because he knows that only in concrete obedience do we become free to believe.

And if you hand us the heavy cup, the bitter one,
of sorrow, filled to the highest brim,
then we take it thankfully, without trembling,
from your good and loving hand.[1]

Dietrich Bonhoeffer

❖ ❖ ❖

As he was walking along, he saw Levi son of
Alphaeus sitting at the tax booth, and he said to
him, "Follow me." And he got up and followed
him.

Mark 2:14

The Way of Love for Human Beings

Christ's time of passion begins not with Holy Week but with the first day of his preaching. His renunciation of the empire as a kingdom of this world takes place not at Golgotha but at the very beginning. And our story is supposed to give expression to this idea (Luke 4:5–8). Jesus could have been Lord of this world. As the Messiah the Jews had dreamed of, he could have freed Israel and led it to fame and honor. He is a remarkable man, who is offered dominion over the world even before the beginning of his ministry. And it is even more remarkable that he turns down this offer. . . .

He knows that for this dominion he would have to pay a price that is too high for him. It would come at the cost of obedience to God's will. . . . He remains the free Son of God and recognizes the devil, who wants to enslave him. "Worship the Lord your God, and serve only him" (Luke 4:8). Jesus knows what that means. It means lowliness, abuse, persecution. It means remaining misunderstood. It means hate, death, the cross. And he chooses this way from the beginning. It is the way of obedience and the way of freedom, for it is the way of God. And therefore it is also the way of love for human beings.

❖   ❖   ❖

You must know that I still have never regretted for a moment my return in 1939, nor anything which then followed. It all happened in full daylight and with good conscience. The fact that I sit here now [in prison] I reckon also as participation in the fate of Germany, to which I committed myself.[2]

Dietrich Bonhoeffer to Eberhard Bethge

Let the same mind be in you that was in Christ Jesus,
  who, though he was in the form of God,
    did not regard equality with God
    as something to be exploited,
  but emptied himself,
    taking the form of a slave,
    being born in human likeness.
  And being found in human form,
    he humbled himself
    and became obedient to the point of death —
    even death on a cross.

Philippians 2:5–8

The Gospel Is Not a Cheap
Consolation of Faith

The cross is not misfortune and hard fate. It is instead the suffering that comes to us from being bound to Jesus Christ. The cross is not accidental, but necessary suffering. The cross is not suffering bound up with natural existence, but suffering bound up with being a Christian. The cross is essentially not just suffering but suffering and being rejected—and also, strictly speaking, being rejected for Jesus Christ's sake, not because of some other kind of behavior or confession. A Christianity that no longer took discipleship seriously, that made of the gospel only a cheap consolation of faith and for which, otherwise, natural and Christian existence were indistinguishably mixed, would have to understand the cross as daily misfortune, as the urgency and anxiety of our natural life. . . . To be cast out in suffering, to be despised and abandoned by people, as is the unending lament of the Psalmist (Ps. 69:7–8), this essential mark of the suffering of the cross can no longer be comprehended by a Christianity that does not know how to distinguish ordinary and Christian existence. The cross means suffering along with Christ.

❖ ❖ ❖

People who want a real relationship with God must stoop from sorrow and be penitent during their time spent on earth. Those who are pure and who love God in absolute loyalty are much oppressed and suffer much holy sorrow. With their ever-available loving hearts, they bow before God and bend down under all this pain and are lower than all the other creatures on earth. Pride is rare among them.[3]

Mechthild of Magdeburg,
"The Flowing Light of the Godhead"

❖   ❖   ❖

"The Son of Man must undergo great suffering, and be rejected by the elders, chief priests, and scribes, and be killed, and on the third day be raised."

Luke 9:22

The Misuse of Vicarious Living

Only in the complete dedication of one's own life to other people is there vicarious living and responsibility. Only the selfless person *lives* responsibly, and that means that only the selfless person lives. Where the divine yes and no become one in a person, life is lived responsibly. . . . A misuse of the vicarious life threatens from two sides: through making one's own self absolute and through making other people absolute. . . . In both cases the origin, essence, and aim of the responsible life in Jesus Christ is denied, and responsibility becomes a self-made abstract idol.

The only thing that bothers me or would bother me is the thought that you are being tormented by anxiety about me, and are not sleeping or eating properly. Forgive me for causing you so much worry.[4]

Dietrich Bonhoeffer to his parents,
14 April 1943

❖   ❖   ❖

Do nothing from selfish ambition or conceit, but in humility regard others as better than yourselves.

Philippians 2:3

Self-Denial Means Knowing Only Christ

If any want to become my followers, let them deny themselves." Just as in denying Christ Peter said, "I do not know the man" [Matt. 26:74], so also should each disciple say this to himself or herself. Self-denial can never be defined as some profusion—be it ever so great—of individual acts of self-torment or asceticism. . . . Self-denial means knowing only Christ, and no longer oneself. It means seeing only Christ, who goes ahead of us, and no longer the path that is too difficult for us. Again, self-denial is saying only: He goes ahead of us; hold fast to him.[5]

Dietrich Bonhoeffer, *The Cost of Discipleship*

What is not a matter of course is that I'm all right here in spite of everything, that I can experience pleasures of one kind or another, and that with it all I keep my spirits up—and so I'm very thankful every day.[6]

Dietrich Bonhoeffer to his parents,
9 November 1943

❖ ❖ ❖

Then he began to curse, and he swore an oath, "I do not know the man!" At that moment the cock crowed. Then Peter remembered what Jesus had said: "Before the cock crows, you will deny me three times." And he went out and wept bitterly.

Matthew 26:74–75

The Yoke That Makes the Burden Light

Take my yoke upon you, and learn from me ..." (Matt. 11:28-30). A yoke is itself a burden, one burden added to another, and yet it has the peculiar nature of making another burden light. A burden that would simply push a person down to the ground becomes bearable through the yoke. . . . Jesus wants to put us human beings under such a yoke, so that our burden will not become too heavy for us. "My yoke" he calls it — that is, the yoke under which he has learned to carry his burden, which is a thousand times heavier than our burden, precisely because it is indeed all of our burdens that he bears. . . .

Those who carry this yoke, and thus learn from him, have a great promise: " . . . *you will find rest for your souls."*

That is the end. This rest is the last thing, and it is already here under the yoke of Jesus. It is yoked together with him in gentleness and humility. But only there where all burdens fall will we find the complete rest that we long for.

❖ ❖ ❖

God lets himself be pushed out of the world and onto the cross; God is impotent and weak in the world yet specifically and only so that he is with us and helps us.[7]

Dietrich Bonhoeffer, *The Mystery of Easter*

❖   ❖   ❖

It is for your sake that I have borne reproach,
that shame has covered my face.

Psalm 69:7

Forgoing the Pious Self

First, we must completely forget how to say, "I will," until God, through the Holy Spirit, teaches us to say it in a new and right way. It is precisely in matters of piety that "I will" can wreak the greatest havoc: "I will be godly, I will be holy, I will keep the commandments." We must first have a basic understanding that in these things, it is not our will but God's will alone that matters. We must also forgo our pious self, so that God can do his work in us. Otherwise our "I will" will almost certainly be followed by bankruptcy. But when through God's grace we have stopped saying, "I will," when through God's new beginning with us in Jesus Christ we have been brought onto his path—in spite of our "I will" and "I won't"—then the Holy Spirit begins to speak in us, and we say something quite new and different from our previous "I will."

The desire for one's own honor hinders faith. One who seeks his own honor is no longer seeking God and his neighbor. What does it matter if I suffer injustice?[8]

Dietrich Bonhoeffer, *Life Together*

I do not understand my own actions. For I do not do what I want, but I do the very thing I hate. Now if I do what I do not want, I agree that the law is good. But in fact it is no longer I that do it, but sin that dwells within me.

Romans 7:15–17

TEMPTATION

In the Wilderness

The Gospels report that Jesus was led by the Spirit into the wilderness to be tempted by the devil (Matt. 4:1). So the temptation does not begin with the Father arming the Son with all powers and weapons, so that he can win the battle. No, the Spirit leads Jesus into the wilderness, into solitude, into forsakenness. God removes from his Son all human and creaturely help. The hour of temptation is supposed to find Jesus weak, alone, and hungry. God leaves human beings alone in temptation. . . .

What must remain incomprehensible to all human, ethical, and religious thought is that in temptation God does not reveal himself as the one who is gracious and near, who arms us with all gifts of the Spirit. Rather, God forsakes us and is quite distant from us. We are in the wilderness.

I'm sure I never realized as clearly as I do here what the Bible and Luther mean by "temptation." Quite suddenly, and for no apparent physical or psychological reason, the peace and composure that were supporting one are jarred. . . . It feels like an invasion from outside, as if by evil powers trying to rob one of what is most vital.[1]

Dietrich Bonhoeffer to his parents
from Tegel prison, 15 May 1943

No one, when tempted, should say, "I am being tempted by God"; for God cannot be tempted by evil and he himself tempts no one. But one is tempted by one's own desire, being lured and enticed by it; then, when that desire has conceived, it gives birth to sin, and that sin, when it is fully grown, gives birth to death. Do not be deceived, my beloved.

James 1:13–16

Lead Us Not into Temptation

Then does the hour of temptation have to come? Is it therefore permissible to pray in this way? Should we not simply pray that in the hour of temptation—which must surely come—we will be given the strength to overcome it? This idea claims to know more about temptation than Christ and to be more pious than the one who experienced the greatest temptation. . . .

Does God have to allow Satan to have so much power? And who are we that we can talk about the idea that temptation *must* come? Do we sit on the divine council of God? And if temptation must indeed come—by virtue of a *divine* "must" that is incomprehensible to us—then Christ, the most tempted of all, calls us to pray against this divine necessity, not to deliver ourselves to temptation in a stoic, resigned fashion, but rather to flee from that dark necessity in which God submits his will to the devil, to appeal to that apparent divine freedom in which God treads the devil under foot. Lead us *not* into temptation! (Matt. 6:13 KJV)

"Be glad. Celebrate! Lose your mindless fear, and take courage today. No, don't ever be afraid, no matter what's happened to you before. That's right, don't be afraid, no matter what you may see coming. Take courage because Christ was crucified for you."[2]

Catherine of Siena, *Letters*

❖ ❖ ❖

"Pray then in this way:
Our Father in heaven,
    hallowed be your name.
Your kingdom come.
Your will be done,
    on earth as it is in heaven.
Give us this day our daily bread.
And forgive us our debts,
    as we also have forgiven our debtors.
And do not bring us to the time of trial,
    but rescue us from the evil one."

Matthew 6:9–13

Conscience Is Shame before God

Before the fall there was no conscience. Not until their separation from their Creator are human beings separated from themselves. And indeed this is the function of conscience: to drive one into flight from God in order, on the one hand, to concede against one's will that God is right and, on the other, to let one feel secure in this flight . . . Conscience drives people away from God and into safe hiding. Here, away from God, they then play the judge themselves and in this way avoid God's judgment. Human beings now really live by their own good and evil, by their deepest separation within themselves. Conscience is shame before God, in which, at the same time, one's own evil is hidden, one justifies oneself, and—against one's own will—reference to the Other is contained. Conscience is not the voice of God in sinful human beings, but defense against this voice, which, however—precisely as defense against one's knowledge and will—still points to this voice.

❖ ❖ ❖

Christ restores all this as God originally intended it to be, without the distortion resulting from our sins.[3]

Dietrich Bonhoeffer to Eberhard Bethge,
18 December 1943

❖   ❖   ❖

Come now, let us argue it out,
　　says the LORD:
though your sins are like scarlet,
　　they shall be like snow;
though they are red like crimson,
　　they shall become like wool.

Isaiah 1:18

Our Inner Power of Resistance

We have been silent witnesses to evil deeds. We have been washed with many waters and have learned the arts of pretence and ambiguous speech. Through experience we have become mistrusting of people and often have not been truthful and honest with them. Through unbearable conflicts we have become worn out and perhaps even cynical—are we still useful? We will need not geniuses, not cynics, not misanthropes, not refined tacticians, but plain, simple, straightforward people. Will our inner power of resistance against what is forced upon us remain strong enough and our uprightness against ourselves ruthless enough for us to find again the path to simplicity and straightforwardness?

❖　❖　❖

Although we are not Christ, if we want to be Christians we must participate in Christ's own magnanimous heart by engaging in responsible action that seizes the hour in complete freedom, facing the danger.[4]

Dietrich Bonhoeffer,
"After Ten Years," 1942

❖   ❖   ❖

He has told you, O mortal, what is good;
and what does the LORD require of you
but to do justice, and to love kindness,
and to walk humbly with your God?

Micah 6:8

Do Not Repay Evil with Evil

D o not raise your hand to strike. Do not open your mouth in anger, but remain still. How can the one who wants to do evil things against you hurt you? It does not hurt you; it hurts the other person. Suffering injustice does not hurt the Christian, but doing injustice does. Indeed, evil can only do one thing to you, namely, make you also become evil. If it does, then it wins. Therefore, do not repay evil with evil. . . .

How can we overcome evil? By our forgiving it endlessly. How does that happen? By our seeing enemies as they really are: as people for whom Christ died, as people Christ loves.

And now, Eberhard, good-bye. . . . And if it should be decided that we are not to meet again, let us remember each other to the end in thankfulness and forgiveness. . . . [5]

> Dietrich Bonhoeffer to Eberhard Bethge,
> 18 November 1943

❖   ❖   ❖

Then Peter came and said to him, "Lord, if another member of the church sins against me, how often should I forgive? As many as seven times?" Jesus said to him, "Not seven times, but, I tell you, seventy-seven times."

> Matthew 18:21–22

The Call to Discipleship
Means Death and Life

Because Jesus' call to the rich young man brings that man's death, because only as one who has died to his own will can he follow Jesus, because Jesus' commandment always means that we must die with all our wishes and all our desires, and because we cannot want our own death — for all these reasons, Jesus Christ in his word must be our death and our life. The call to discipleship, or baptism in the name of Jesus Christ, means death and life. Christ's call, or baptism, means placing the Christian into a daily struggle against sin and the devil. Hence every new day, with its temptations through flesh and the world, brings new sufferings of Jesus Christ upon his disciples.[6]

Dietrich Bonhoeffer, *The Cost of Discipleship*

Discipleship is commitment to the suffering Christ. This is why the suffering of Christians is nothing disconcerting. Rather, it is pure blessing and joy.[7]

Dietrich Bonhoeffer, *The Cost of Discipleship*

❖   ❖   ❖

He called the crowd with his disciples, and said to them, "If any want to become my followers, let them deny themselves and take up their cross and follow me. For those who want to save their life will lose it, and those who lose their life for my sake, and for the sake of the gospel, will save it."

Mark 8:34–35

We Watch with Christ in Gethsemane

It is in the complete this-worldliness of life that we must first learn how to believe. When we have fully renounced making something out of ourselves—be it a saint or a converted sinner or a church man or woman (a so-called priestly figure!), a righteous or an unrighteous person, a sick or a healthy person—when we have renounced all of that, we fall completely into God's arms and what I call this-worldliness, namely, living in an abundance of tasks, questions, successes and failures, experiences, and helplessness. We then take seriously no longer our own suffering, but the suffering of God in the world. We watch with Christ in Gethsemane. This, I think, is faith.

One thing remains clear or at least sensed: doubt and temptation about the meaningfulness of being cast to and fro, of being at the mercy of things, will not cease as long as we remain focused on ourselves, as long as in one form or another "the other" does not step into our lives.[8]

Dietrich Bonhoeffer to Detlef Albers,
30 August 1929

❖　❖　❖

In his anguish he prayed more earnestly, and his sweat became like great drops of blood falling down on the ground. When he got up from prayer, he came to the disciples and found them sleeping because of grief, and he said to them, "Why are you sleeping? Get up and pray that you may not come into the time of trial."

Luke 22:44–46

THE PURPOSE
OF SUFFERING

A Great Capacity for Suffering

I t must be clear to us that most people learn only through personal experience occurring to their own bodies. *First*, this explains why most people are remarkably incapable of any sort of preventative action. We keep thinking that we ourselves will be spared when disaster strikes—until it is too late. *Second*, it explains our insensitivity to the suffering of others; solidarity with suffering arises in proportion to our own increasing fear of imminent doom. . . . We are not responsible for all the injustice and suffering in the world, nor do we wish to judge the whole world. Psychologically, our lack of imagination, sensitivity, and inner readiness is balanced by a kind of unwavering calmness, an undisturbed ability to work, and a great capacity for suffering.[1]

Dietrich Bonhoeffer, "After Ten Years," 1942

This is my second Passiontide here. When people suggest in their letters . . . that I'm "suffering" here, I reject the thought. It seems to me a profanation. These things mustn't be dramatized. I doubt very much whether I'm "suffering" any more than you, or most people, are suffering today. Of course, a great deal here is horrible, but where isn't it? . . . No, suffering must be something quite different, and have a quite different dimension, from what I've so far experienced.[2]

Letter to Eberhard Bethge
from Tegel prison, 9 March 1944

Therefore, to keep me from being too elated, a thorn was given me in the flesh, a messenger of Satan to torment me, to keep me from being too elated. Three times I appealed to the Lord about this, that it would leave me, but he said to me, "My grace is sufficient for you, for power is made perfect in weakness." So, I will boast all the more gladly of my weaknesses, so that the power of Christ may dwell in me. Therefore I am content with weaknesses, insults, hardships, persecutions, and calamities for the sake of Christ; for whenever I am weak, then I am strong.

2 Corinthians 12:7–10

The View from Below

It is an experience of incomparable value that we have learned to see the great events of world history from below, from the perspective of the excluded, the suspect, the poorly treated, the powerless, the oppressed, and the ridiculed — in short, those who suffer. Only if bitterness and suffering have not eaten up our heart, can we then see with new eyes the great and the small, fortune and misfortune, strength and weakness. Our view of greatness, humanity, right, and mercy has become clearer, freer, and more incorruptible. And for observing and actively exploring the world, personal suffering has become a more useful key, a more fruitful principle, than personal fortune. It all depends on our not letting this perspective from below make us biased in favor of the eternally unsatisfied. Rather, out of a higher satisfaction that is actually grounded from beyond — beyond below and above — we must do justice to life in all its dimensions and in that way affirm life.

My dear Dietrich,

I don't know whether I shall be allowed to send you this greeting, but I want to try. The bells outside are ringing for worship, and memories flood back to the marvelous, profound hours that we spent together in the garrison church, and those many joyful, happy, untroubled Easters with children, parents, brothers and sisters. . . . You cannot know how much it oppresses me that I am the cause of this suffering that you, Christel, the children, our parents now undergo; that because of me, my dear wife and you have been deprived of freedom.[3]

Hans von Dohnanyi to Dietrich Bonhoeffer,
Good Friday, 23 April 1943

❖ ❖ ❖

When he came to Nazareth, where he had been brought up, he went to the synagogue on the sabbath day, as was his custom. He stood up to read, and the scroll of the prophet Isaiah was given to him. He unrolled the scroll and found the place where it was written:
"The Spirit of the Lord is upon me,
because he has anointed me
to bring good news to the poor.
He has sent me to proclaim release to the captives
and recovery of sight to the blind,
to let the oppressed go free,
to proclaim the year of the Lord's favor."

Luke 4:16–19

God Is a God of Bearing

Suffering must be borne, so that it will pass. Either the world must bear it and go down because of it, or it falls on Christ and is overcome in him. So Christ suffers vicariously for the world. . . . God is a God of bearing. The Son of God bore our flesh, and for that reason he bore the cross; he bore all our sins and through his bearing achieved reconciliation. So too are disciples called to be bearers. Being a Christian consists in bearing.

Give me strength to bear what you send,
and do not let fear rule over me.[3]

> Dietrich Bonhoeffer,
> "Prayers in Times of Distress"

❖ ❖ ❖

Love is patient; love is kind; love is not envious
or boastful or arrogant or rude. It does not insist
on its own way; it is not irritable or resentful; it
does not rejoice in wrongdoing, but rejoices in the
truth. It bears all things, believes all things, hopes
all things, endures all things.

> 1 Corinthians 13:4–7

Suffering and Being Rejected

Death on the cross means suffering and dying as one who is rejected and cast out. Jesus must suffer and be rejected by virtue of divine necessity. Any attempt to interfere with what is necessary is satanic—even and precisely when it comes out of the circle of the disciples, for it does not want to let Christ be Christ. . . . Thus for Jesus it now becomes necessary to relate the "must" of suffering to his disciples in a clear and unambiguous way. As Christ is Christ only as the suffering and rejected one, so the disciple is a disciple only as one who suffers and is rejected, as one crucified with Jesus. Discipleship, understood as being bound to the person of Jesus Christ, places the disciple under the law of Christ, that is, under the cross.

❖　❖　❖

It was Maria's birthday on Good Friday. If I didn't know how courageously she bore the death of her father, her brother and two beloved cousins last year, I should be really concerned about her. She'll now have the consolation of Easter and the support of her numerous family, and her Red Cross work will keep her fully occupied. Give her my fond love and tell her that she mustn't be sad, but as brave as she has always been. She's still so young, that's the hard part.[5]

Dietrich Bonhoeffer to his parents
from Tegel prison, 25 April 1943

The saying is sure:
If we have died with him, we will also live with him;
if we endure, we will also reign with him;
if we deny him, he will also deny us;
if we are faithless, he remains faithful —
for he cannot deny himself.

2 Timothy 2:11–13

Participation in the Suffering of God

S o, you could not stay awake with me one hour?" [Jesus asked in Gethsemane] (Matt. 26:40b). That is the opposite of everything that the religious person expects from God. Human beings are called to share the suffering of God in a godless world. Therefore we must really live in the godless world and may not make the attempt somehow to conceal, to transfigure its godlessness religiously; we must live in a "worldly" way and in just this way participate in God's suffering. . . . It is not the religious act that makes the Christian, but participation in the suffering of God in the life of the world. This is the reversal: not to think first of our own needs, questions, sins, and anxieties, but to let ourselves be pulled into the way of Jesus, into the messianic event that is now fulfilled (Isa. 53:4–5).

And how shall we pray those psalms of unspeakable misery and suffering, the meaning of which we have hardly begun to sense even remotely? We can and we should pray the psalms of suffering, the psalms of the passion, not in order to generate in ourselves what our hearts do not know of their own experience, not to make our own laments, but because all this suffering was real and actual in Jesus Christ.[6]

Dietrich Bonhoeffer, *Life Together*

Surely he has borne our infirmities
    and carried our diseases;
yet we accounted him stricken,
    struck down by God, and afflicted.
But he was wounded for our transgressions,
    crushed for our iniquities;
upon him was the punishment that made us whole,
    and by his bruises we are healed.

Isaiah 53:4–5

Suffering Produces Patience

S uffering produces patience" (Rom. 5:3 Luther).
Translated literally, patience means holding the course, not throwing off the burden but
bearing it. Today we in the church know all too
little about the real blessing of bearing. Bearing,
not shaking off; bearing, but also not collapsing;
bearing as Christ bore the cross, staying under,
and there below, finding Christ. . . . Experience
produces hope. For every attack withstood is
already the prelude to the final victory; every conquered wave brings us closer to the land we long
for. Therefore, hope grows with experience, and
in the experience of tribulation a reflection of the
eternal glory can already be perceived.

In suffering, the deliverance consists in our being allowed to put the matter out of our own hands into God's hands.[7]

Dietrich Bonhoeffer to Eberhard Bethge,
28 July 1944

❖ ❖ ❖

And not only that, but we also boast in our sufferings, knowing that suffering produces endurance, and endurance produces character, and character produces hope, and hope does not disappoint us, because God's love has been poured into our hearts through the Holy Spirit that has been given to us.

Romans 5:3–5

Why Have You Forgotten Me?

W hy have you forgotten me?" (Ps. 42:9). This question comes from the lips of all Christians when everything stands against them, when all earthly hope has been shattered, when in the course of great world events they feel totally lost, when all of life's goals seem unattainable, and everything appears pointless. . . . When I fall into doubt, God remains solid as a rock. When I waver, God remains unshakable. When I become unfaithful, God becomes faithful. . . . To endure humiliation and to be mocked for the sake of the faith—that has been a distinction of the godly for centuries. It hurts body and soul that no day passes without the name of God being doubted and blasphemed. Where, then, is your God? I confess God before the world and before all enemies of God when in deepest need I believe in God's goodness, when in guilt I believe in forgiveness, when in death I believe in life, when in defeat I believe in victory, when in desolation I believe in God's gracious presence. Those who have found God in the cross of Jesus Christ know how wonderfully God hides himself in this world and how he is closest precisely when we believe him to be most distant.

❖ ❖ ❖

[The lamentation Psalms] proclaim Jesus Christ to be the only help in suffering, for in him God is with us.[8]

Dietrich Bonhoeffer, *Psalms*

❖ ❖ ❖

My God, my God, why have you forsaken me?
Why are you so far from helping me, from the words
    of my groaning?
O my God, I cry by day, but you do not answer;
    and by night, but find no rest.

Psalm 22:1–2

THE CROSS

Without Any Illusion

As the New Testament proclaims life to the dying, as life and death collide in the cross of Christ, and as life swallows up death—only when we see this do we believe in the church under the cross. Only when we look at reality with clear eyes, without any illusion about our morality or our culture, can we believe. Otherwise our faith becomes an illusion. . . . [Believers] do not believe in people or in the good in people that ultimately must triumph; they also do not believe in the church in its human power. Rather, believers believe solely in God, who creates and does the impossible, who creates life out of death, who has called the dying church to life against and in spite of us and through us. But God does it alone.

❖　❖　❖

If you need love, God's the love you need because
the power of His love kept Him nailed fast to the
cross. Only the power of love kept the God-man
bound there, not mere cross and nails.[1]

Catherine of Siena, *Letters*

❖   ❖   ❖

Listen, I will tell you a mystery! We will not all
die, but we will all be changed, in a moment, in the
twinkling of an eye, at the last trumpet. For the
trumpet will sound, and the dead will be raised
imperishable, and we will be changed.

1 Corinthians 15:51–52

His Yoke and Burden Are the Cross

Jesus calls all who are laden with many kinds of suffering and burdens to cast off their yoke and take upon themselves his yoke, which is easy, and his burden, which is light (Matt. 11:30). His yoke and his burden are the cross. To walk under this cross is not misery and despair but refreshment and rest for the soul. It is the greatest joy. Here we are no longer under self-made laws and burdens but are under the yoke of the one who knows us and who walks with us himself, under the yoke. Under his yoke we are certain of this nearness and communion. It is he himself whom disciples find when they take up their cross.

❖ ❖ ❖

A king who dies on the cross must be the king of a rather strange kingdom. Only those who understand the profound paradox of the cross can also understand the whole meaning of Jesus' assertion: my kingdom is not of this world.[2]

Dietrich Bonhoeffer,
"Lectures to the Congregation in Barcelona"

❖ ❖ ❖

"Come to me, all you that are weary and are carrying heavy burdens, and I will give you rest. Take my yoke upon you, and learn from me; for I am gentle and humble in heart, and you will find rest for your souls. For my yoke is easy, and my burden is light."

Matthew 1:28–30

Jesus' Love Is Love
That Takes upon Itself the Cross

The love of Jesus Christ for us — what is that? To us, is it only a word? Or have we experienced it? Only those who have experienced it can, in turn, love others with this love. Jesus' love — that is love that comes from eternity and leads toward eternity. It does not cling to temporal things but surrounds us, because we are supposed to be eternal. It lets nothing stop it, for it is God's eternal faithfulness to us. Jesus' love — that is love that shrinks from no pain, no renunciation, no suffering, if it helps the other person. It is the love with which he loved us solely for our person. It is the love with which he loved us solely for our own sake, with which on earth he took upon himself mockery and hatred and died on the cross. Jesus' love is love that takes upon itself the cross. Jesus' love — that is love that is for us as we are. As a mother loves her child as it is — and the greater the need, the greater the love, because she knows that the child requires her love — such is the love of Jesus for us. He accepts us as we are.

Even today I can believe the love of God and forgive my enemies only by going back to the cross
of Christ, to the carrying out of the wrath of God.
The cross of Jesus is valid for all.[3]

Dietrich Bonhoeffer, *Psalms*

❖   ❖   ❖

"I give you a new commandment, that you love one
another. Just as I have loved you, you also should
love one another. By this everyone will know that you
are my disciples, if you have love for one another."

John 13:34–35

Where the Cross Stands,
the Resurrection Is Near

Christ goes through the cross, only through the cross, to life, to the resurrection, to victory? That, indeed, is the marvelous—and yet for many people so repulsive—theme of the Bible, that the only visible sign of God in the world is the cross. Christ is not gloriously transported from earth into heaven. He must instead go to the cross. And precisely there, where the cross stands, the resurrection is near. Precisely here, where all lose faith in God, where all despair about the power of God, God is fully there, and Christ is alive and near. Where one stands on a razor's edge of becoming an apostate or remaining true, God and Christ are fully there. Where the power of darkness wants to overcome the light of God, there God triumphs and judges the darkness.

So much could change, if people really believed this.[4]

Dietrich Bonhoeffer to Eberhard Bethge
from Tegel prison, 25 March 1944

❖   ❖   ❖

Therefore, since we are surrounded by so great a cloud of witnesses, let us also lay aside every weight and the sin that clings so closely, and let us run with perseverance the race that is set before us, looking to Jesus the pioneer and perfecter of our faith, who for the sake of the joy that was set before him endured the cross, disregarding its shame, and has taken his seat at the right hand of the throne of God. Consider him who endured such hostility against himself from sinners, so that you may not grow weary or lose heart.

Hebrews 12:1–3

HOLY WEEK

The Way to the Cross

We have come again to Passiontide, and again we must collect our thoughts that we may understand what it means. . . .

Jesus knows what that means. It means debasement, revilement, persecution. It means being misunderstood. It means hatred, death, the cross. And he chooses this way from the very outset. It is the way of obedience and the way of freedom, for it is the way of God. . . . And we are going with him, as individuals and as the church. We are the church beneath the cross, that is, in disguise. Yet here as well, all we can do is realize that our kingdom, too, is not of this world.[1]

Dietrich Bonhoeffer, devotional at Berlin,
Technical University, Passiontide 1932

❖ ❖ ❖

This isn't the third sheet I've written you, it's the sixth. I kept trying to tell you about Easter, about Maundy Thursday Mass and the celebration of the hour of Christ's death on Good Friday, about the sermon on the Descent into Hell, and finally about Easter Eve, but I simply couldn't. . . . I found the whole thing strange and fundamentally incomprehensible, as you can tell, but I did, for all that, sense the existence of some immense inherent force, and it frightens me because it's so new and great and unfathomable.[2]

Maria von Wedemeyer to Dietrich Bonhoeffer,
11 April 1944

As he rode along, people kept spreading their cloaks on the road. As he was now approaching the path down from the Mount of Olives, the whole multitude of the disciples began to praise God joyfully with a loud voice for all the deeds of power that they had seen, saying,
    "Blessed is the king
        who comes in the name of the Lord!
    Peace in heaven,
        and glory in the highest heaven!"

Luke 19:36–38

If There Were No Resurrection

I f God's history among human beings had come to an end on Good Friday, the last word on humankind would be: guilt, revolt, unfitting of all human-titanic powers, storming of heaven by human beings, godlessness, abandonment by God, which ends up ultimately in meaninglessness and despair. "Then your faith is futile. Then you are still in your sins. Then we are the most miserable of human beings." That is, the last word spoken is: humankind. On the cross of Jesus Christ, not only does our moral and religious life come to ruin by being found guilty, but our entire culture is also judged.[3]

Dietrich Bonhoeffer, sermon in Barcelona
for Easter Sunday, 8 April 1928

❖   ❖   ❖

Christian life means being human by virtue of the incarnation, it means being judged and pardoned by virtue of the cross, and means to live a new life in the power of the resurrection. None of these becomes real without the others.[4]

Dietrich Bonhoeffer, *Ethics*

❖　❖　❖

If Christ has not been raised, your faith is futile and you are still in your sins.

1 Corinthians 15:17

The Reconciliation of the World with God

Those who look at Jesus Christ in actuality see God and the world in one. From now on, they can no longer see God without seeing the world, nor the human without seeing God. *Ecce homo* — see what a human being! In him the reconciliation of the world with God took place. The world is conquered not through smashing it but through reconciliation. Not ideals, programs, not conscience, duty, responsibility, virtue, but the perfect love of God all alone can meet reality and overcome it. It is not a general idea of love, but the love of God really lived in Jesus Christ, that accomplishes that. This love of God for the world does not withdraw from reality back into noble souls transported away from the world but rather experiences and suffers the reality of the world in the severest way. The world amuses itself with the body of Jesus Christ, but the martyred One forgives the world its sin. This is how reconciliation takes place.

"Remember, I am with you" . . . that is the Easter message, not the distant, but the near God, that is Easter.[5]

Dietrich Bonhoeffer,
sermon in Barcelona, 15 April 1928

And remember, I am with you always, to the end of the age.

Matthew 28:20b

Our Entire Life Depends on Easter

Easter, with the joy of the coming of spring, with all the happiness with which the sun warms our hearts, has become for each of us since childhood a festival dear to our hearts, a festival filled with warm memories from which we do not want to part. Who among us would want to lose even a single spring from our lives? But to say that our entire life depends on Easter, that our existence would be threatened if there were no Easter—who among us would want or even could bear such a thing? But Paul did indeed say it. And because he reflected a bit more thoroughly on this question than we tend to do, we may assume that such a statement does indeed harbor a certain meaning about which one might perhaps reflect further. "If Christ has not been raised, your faith is futile."[6]

Dietrich Bonhoeffer, sermon on 1 Corinthians 14:17
in Barcelona, Easter Sunday 1928

On Wednesday of Holy Week, I was meditating on the death of the Son of God incarnate. I was trying to empty my soul of everything else so I could be more focused on His Passion. Suddenly, a divine word announced in my soul, "My love for you is not a hoax." These words cut me deeply because I saw how true they were. I saw His acts of love and everything the Son of God ever did and suffered, and they revealed that His love for me was no "hoax." I saw God had loved me better and more intimately than anyone else ever could or had.[7]

Angela of Foligno, *Instructions*

But in fact Christ has been raised from the dead, the first fruits of those who have died. For since death came through a human being, the resurrection of the dead has also come through a human being; for as all die in Adam, so all will be made alive in Christ.

1 Corinthians 15:20–21

One of You Will Betray Me

Jesus had kept one secret from his disciples until the Last Supper (Matt. 26:20–25). It is true that he had not left them in the dark about his path of suffering, but he had still not revealed to them the deepest secret. Only in the hour of their last fellowship in their Holy Communion could he say to them: The Son of Man will be handed over into the hands of sinners—through betrayal. "One of you will betray me."

By themselves, his enemies can gain no power over him. It is up to a friend, a very close friend, to hand him over; it is a disciple who betrays him. The most fearful event does not happen from the outside but from within. Jesus' path to Golgotha has its beginning in a disciple's betrayal. While some sleep that incomprehensible sleep in Gethsemane (Matt. 26:40), one betrays him. In the end "all the disciples deserted him and fled" (Matt. 26:56).

❖   ❖   ❖

Who is this Judas? Who is the betrayer? Faced with this question, are we capable of more than asking with the disciples: "Surely not I, Lord?"[8]

Dietrich Bonhoeffer, sermon in Finkenwalde,
14 March 1937

❖ ❖ ❖

Now the betrayer had given them a sign, saying, "The one I will kiss is the man; arrest him." At once he came up to Jesus and said, "Greetings, Rabbi!" and kissed him. Jesus said to him, "Friend, do what you are here to do." Then they came and laid hands on Jesus and arrested him.

Matthew 26:48–50

All Hope Dashed?

"Father, into your hands I commend my spirit" (Luke 23:46), Jesus prays aloud. "It is finished," and with that he bows his head and dies (John 19:30). It had all happened the way it had to happen. The love of God had appeared on earth in humiliation, shame, and disgrace. On the cross the wrath of God slew his own Son for the wickedness of the world, for the wickedness of the world had nailed the Son to the cross. On Good Friday let us not think right away about the fact that with Easter things were given a new direction. We want to think about how with the death of Jesus the disciples saw all hope dashed. Scattered from each other, they brooded in hopeless sorrow about what had happened. Only when we can take the death of Jesus just as seriously as they did, will we rightly understand what the resurrection message can bring.

❖ ❖ ❖

Good Friday and Easter—the days of God's over-powering acts in history, acts in which God's judgment and grace were revealed to all the world—are just around the corner. Judgment in those hours in which Jesus Christ, our Lord, hung on the cross; grace in that hour in which death was swallowed up in victory. It was not human beings who accomplished anything here; no, God alone did it. He came to human beings in infinite love. He judged what is human. And he granted grace beyond any merit.[9]

Dietrich Bonhoeffer, sermon in Barcelona
for the third Sunday in Lent, 11 March 1928

❖　❖　❖

I ask, then, has God rejected his people? By no means! . . . God has not rejected his people whom he foreknew. Do you not know what the scripture says of Elijah, how he pleads with God against Israel? "Lord, they have killed your prophets, they have demolished your altars; I alone am left, and they are seeking my life." But what is the divine reply to him? "I have kept for myself seven thousand who have not bowed the knee to Baal." So too at the present time there is a remnant, chosen by grace. But if it is by grace, it is no longer on the basis of works, otherwise grace would no longer be grace.

Romans 11:1–6

The Empty Tomb, a Puzzle

For the world the empty tomb is an ambiguous historical fact. For believers it is a historical sign of God that follows necessarily from the miracle of the resurrection and confirms it, a sign from the God who deals with human beings in history. There is no historical proof for the resurrection. . . . The decision of the historian in this matter, which remains so scientifically puzzling, will be dictated by the presuppositions of one's worldview. In that respect, however, it loses interest and importance for believers who are grounded in God's acting in history. Thus, for the world there remains an unsolvable puzzle, which in no way can compel faith in the resurrection of Jesus. For believers, however, this puzzle is the sign of the reality about which they already know, a mark of divine activity in history. Scholarship can neither prove nor disprove the resurrection of Jesus, for it is a miracle of God. But faith, to which the resurrected One witnesses as the living One, recognizes in the very testimony of the Scripture the historicity of the resurrection as an action of God, which in its miraculous nature can present itself to science only as a puzzle.

❖ ❖ ❖

Good Friday and Easter free us to think about other things far beyond our own personal fate, about the ultimate meaning of all life, suffering, and events; and we lay hold of a great hope.[10]

Dietrich Bonhoeffer to his parents,
Easter Day, 25 April 1943

❖ ❖ ❖

They took the body of Jesus and wrapped it with the spices in linen cloths, according to the burial custom of the Jews. Now there was a garden in the place where he was crucified, and in the garden there was a new tomb in which no one had ever been laid. And so, because it was the Jewish day of Preparation, and the tomb was nearby, they laid Jesus there.

John 19:40–42

The Easter Message

Easter is not a battle between darkness and light that ultimately must end in the victory of light, because darkness is actually a nothing, because death is indeed already life. Easter is not a battle of winter and spring, of ice and sun. Rather, it is the battle of guilty humanity against divine love—or better: of divine love against guilty humanity, a battle in which God seems to be defeated on Good Friday, but in which God, in his very losing, wins on Easter. . . . Good Friday is not the darkness that necessarily has to yield to light . . . it is the day on which the God who became human, the love that became a person, is killed by the people who want to become gods. . . . Easter is not an immanent—that is, an inner-worldly—event, but a transcendent event that is something above and beyond the world, an inter-vention of God from eternity, by virtue of which God declares his commitment to his Holy One and awakens him from death. Easter is not about immortality but about resurrection from a death that is a real death with all its frightfulness and horrors, resurrection from a death of the body and the soul, of the whole person, resurrection by the power of God's mighty act. This is the Easter message.

❖　❖　❖

Death cannot keep back love; love is stronger than death. The meaning of Good Friday and Easter Sunday is that God's path to human beings leads back to God.[11]

Dietrich Bonhoeffer,
"Lectures to the Congregation in Barcelona"

❖　❖　❖

Mary Magdalene went and announced to the disciples, "I have seen the Lord"; and she told them that he had said these things to her.

John 20:18

NOTES

Editor's Preface

1. Dietrich Bonhoeffer, *I Want to Live These Days with You: A Year of Daily Devotions* (Louisville, KY: Westminster John Knox Press, 2007), 63.

2. Eberhard Bethge, *Dietrich Bonhoeffer: A Biography*, rev. ed. (Minneapolis: Fortress Press, 2000), 260.

3. Stephen R. Haynes and Lori Brandt Hale, *Bonhoeffer for Armchair Theologians* (Louisville, KY: Westminster John Knox Press, 2009), 70–76.

4. H. Fischer-Hüllstrung, "A Report from Flossenbürg," in *I Knew Dietrich Bonhoeffer: Reminiscences by His Friends*, ed.Wolf-Dieter Zimmermann and Ronald Gregor Smith, trans. Käthe Gregor Smith (New York: Harper & Row, 1966), 232, recounted in Eberhard Bethge, *Dietrich Bonhoeffer: A Biography*, rev. ed. (Minneapolis: Fortress Press, 2000), 927–28.

Lent Week One: Prayerful Reflection

1. Dietrich Bonhoeffer, *The Cost of Discipleship*, quoted in Dietrich Bonhoeffer, *Meditations on the Cross* (Louisville, KY: Westminster John Knox Press, 1998), 14.

2. Dietrich Bonhoeffer, *Life Together: The Classic Exploration of Christian Community* (San Francisco: HarperOne, 1954), 29.

3. Dietrich Bonhoeffer, *Psalms: The Prayer Book of the Bible* (Minneapolis: Augsburg Fortress, 1970), 64.

4. Dietrich Bonhoeffer, *Meditating on the Word* (Cambridge, MA: Cowley Publications, 1986), 49.

5. Ruth-Alice von Bismarck and Ulrich Kabitz, *Love Letters from Cell 92: The Correspondence between Dietrich Bonhoeffer and Maria von Wedemeyer 1943–1945* (Nashville: Abingdon, 1992), 17.

6. Dietrich Bonhoeffer, *A Testament to Freedom: The Essential Writings of Dietrich Bonhoeffer*, ed. Geffrey B. Kelly and F. Burton Nelson (San Francisco: HarperOne, 1995), 219.

7. Ibid., 489.

Lent Week Two: Self-Denial

1. Bonhoeffer, *I Want to Live These Days with You*, 382.

2. Bonhoeffer, *Psalms*, 80.

3. Mechthild of Magdeburg, "The Flowing Light of the Godhead," in Carmen Acevedo Butcher, *A Little Daily Wisdom: Christian Women Mystics* (Brewster, MA: Paraclete Press, 2005), 63.

4. Dietrich Bonhoeffer, *Letters & Papers from Prison, New Greatly Enlarged Edition* (New York: Simon & Schuster, 1997), 22.

5. Bonhoeffer, *The Cost of Discipleship*, quoted in Bonhoeffer, *Meditations on the Cross*, 13.

6. Bonhoeffer, *Letters and Papers from Prison*, 126.

7. Dietrich Bonhoeffer, *The Mystery of Easter* (New York: Crossroad Publishing Company), 10.

8. Bonhoeffer, *Life Together*, 95.

Lent Week Three: Temptation

1. Bonhoeffer, *Letters and Papers from Prison*, 39.

2. Catherine of Siena, *Letters*, in Butcher, *A Little Daily Wisdom*, 52.

3. Bonhoeffer, *Letters and Papers from Prison*, 166.

4. Bonhoeffer, "After Ten Years," quoted in *Meditations on the Cross*, 26.

5. Bonhoeffer, *Letters and Papers from Prison*, 131.

6. Bonhoeffer, *The Cost of Discipleship*, quoted in Bonhoeffer, *Meditations on the Cross*, 15.

7. Ibid., 16.

8. Dietrich Bonhoeffer, *Dietrich Bonhoeffer Works*, vol. 10, *Barcelona, Berlin, New York, 1928–1931* (Minneapolis: Fortress Press, 2008), 189.

Lent Week Four: The Purpose of Suffering

1. Bonhoeffer, notes from "After Ten Years," in Bonhoeffer, *Meditations on the Cross*, 25.

2. Bonhoeffer, *Letters and Papers from Prison*, 231–32.

3. Ibid., 24.

4. Ibid., 142.

5. Bonhoeffer, *Love Letters from Cell 92*, 12.

6. Bonhoeffer, *Life Together*, 48.

7. Bonhoeffer, *Letters and Papers from Prison*, 375.

8. Dietrich Bonhoeffer, *Psalms*, 48.

Lent Week Five: The Cross

1. Catherine of Siena, *Letters*, in Butcher, *A Little Daily Wisdom*, 32.

2. Bonhoeffer, "Lectures to the Congregation in Barcelona," in *Dietrich Bonhoeffer Works*, vol. 10, 357.

3. Bonhoeffer, *Psalms*, 59–60.

4. Bonhoeffer, *Mystery of Easter*, 3.

Holy Week

1. Bonhoeffer, devotional at Berlin, Technical University, Passiontide 1932, quoted in Bonhoeffer, *Meditations on the Cross*, 7–8.

2. Bonhoeffer, *Love Letters from Cell 92*, 182–83.

3. Bonhoeffer, sermon on Easter Sunday, Barcelona, April 8, 1928, quoted in Bonhoeffer, *Meditations on the Cross*, 72.

4. Bonhoeffer, "The Ultimate and Penultimate Things," in *Ethics*; quoted in Bonhoeffer, *Meditations on the Cross*, 78.

5. Bonhoeffer, "Sermon on Matthew 28:20, Barcelona, 15 April 1928," in *Dietrich Bonhoeffer Works*, vol. 10, 491.

6. Bonhoeffer, sermon on 1 Corinthians 15:17, Barcelona, Easter Sunday 1928, quoted in *Dietrich Bonhoeffer Works*, vol. 10, 485.

7. Angela of Foligno, *Instructions*, in *A Little Daily Wisdom*, 73.

8. Bonhoeffer, sermon in Finkenwalde, 14 March 1937, quoted in Bonhoeffer, *Meditations on the Cross*, 36.

9. Bonhoeffer, sermon on Romans 11:6, Barcelona, March 11, 1928 (Third Sunday in Lent), quoted in Bonhoeffer, *Meditations on the Cross*, 20.

10. Bonhoeffer, *Letters and Papers from Prison*, 25.

11. Dietrich Bonhoeffer, "Lectures to the Congregation in Barcelona," in *Dietrich Bonhoeffer Works*, vol. 10, 357.

SCRIPTURE INDEX